Middle School
Language Arts Challenge

Written by Phyllis Amerikaner • Illustrated by Kelly Kennedy

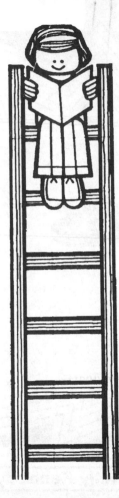

The Learning Works

Edited by Jan Stiles

The purchase of this book entitles the individual teacher to reproduce copies for use in the classroom.

The reproduction of any part for an entire school system or for commercial use is strictly prohibited.

No form of this work may be reproduced or transmitted or recorded without written permission from the publisher.

Copyright © 1994
THE LEARNING WORKS, INC.
P.O. Box 6187
Santa Barbara, CA 93160
All rights reserved.
Printed in the United States of America.

ISBN: 0-88160-272-8

Introduction

Middle School Language Arts Challenge is packed with lively and creative instant activities that can be used in a middle school classroom in a variety of ways:

- class openers
- "problem-of-the-day" challenges
- homework assignments
- supplements to topics covered in class
- skits and role-playing

- extra credit
- motivation for vocabulary building, reading, and research
- classroom bees or contests
- stimulation of originality, creativity, fluency, and flexibility

Middle School Language Arts Challenge contains seven major sections, each filled with activities to enrich the language arts curriculum. The activities relate to

- literature
- creative writing
- journalism and journal writing
- punctuation, grammar, and usage

- vocabulary
- public speaking and drama
- games and challenges to encourage middle school students to be creative and expand their thinking

The format of this book makes it extremely flexible and easy to use. The activities can be reproduced and used with students in the ways listed above, or you can read the activities aloud as "brain-teasers" to get your students thinking. In addition, the activities in the literature and vocabulary sections make ideal cooperative learning exercises.

Middle School Language Arts Challenge provides middle school teachers with activities to motivate, inspire, and otherwise stretch the middle school language arts students in lots of fun and creative ways!

Middle School Language Arts Challenge
© The Learning Works, Inc.

CONTENTS

Literature   8-32

Cast of Characters 8
Villainous Villains .9
Who Said That? 10
Who Am I? 11
Famous Settings .12
Literary Geography 13
Throughout History 14-15
Memorable Leads 16-17
Name That Author 18
Literary Aliases .19
Series of Series 20
Animals in Literature 21
Animal Titles 22
Book Bouquets 23
Devouring a Good Book 24
Colorful Literature 25
Poetic Quotes 26
The Extraordinary Newbery 27
More Newbery 28
Literary Trivia 29-30
Authors with Challenges 31
Odd Jobs 32

Creative Writing   34-44

Ingenious Inventions 34
Four-By-Four Stories 35
Under the Microscope 36
Bigger Than Life 37
The Turning Point 38
See Middle-Earth! 39
Nice To Know You 40
Difficult Dilemmas 41
Snapshot Impressions 42
Foreshadowing .43
In Other Words .44

Contents
(continued)

Journalism and Journal Writing 46-52

Extra! Extra! 46
By-Lines by You 47
A Pivotal Moment 48
Object Lesson 49
Portrait of a Writer 50
Dinner at My House 51
Most-ly Me 52

Punctuation, Grammar, and Usage 54-72

Pesky Apostrophes 54
Periods and Commas 55
A Plethora of Plurals 56
A Capital Idea 57
Misplaced Modifiers 58
They're, Their, There 59
In Agreement 60
Agreeable Pronouns 61
Regularly Irregular 62-63
Proofreader's Symbols 64
Proof It 65

Sentence Diagram Models 66
Dynamite Diagrams 67
Parts-of-Speech Stories 68
Parts-of-Speech Story I 69-70
Parts-of-Speech Story II 71
Parts-of-Speech Story III 72

Vocabulary 74-88

Artistic Vocabulary 74
Worldly Word Origins 75
Namesakes 76
Occupations 77
The Hobbyist 78
Don't Mispell Misspell It 79
Don't Myth Out 80-81
Daffy Definitions 82
Anagrams 83
Syllable Stretch 84
Say "Aa" 85
Measured Words 86
A Good Reading Vocabulary 87
Food for Thought 88

Middle School Language Arts Challenge
© The Learning Works, Inc.

Contents
(continued)

Public Speaking and Drama	90-100
Instant Debates	.90
What If?	.91
Improv	.92-93
Ideas For Improv Situations	.94
Ideas For Improv Actions	.95
Extemporaneous Skits	.96-97
Future Digs	.98
What's My Bag?	.99
Power of Persuasion	.100

Games and Challenges	102-114
Decipher	.102
Rail Fence Code	.103
Ever, Ever Eve	.104
Reversals	.105
It's Symbolic	.106-107
Lists of Lists	.108
What's in a Name?	.109
The Union Jack	.110
Pangram Puzzlers	.111
Tom Swiftly	.112
Musical Words	.113
All Groan Up	.114

Answer Key	115-128

Literature

The literary works in this section, by necessity, span a wide range of interest and ability levels. Some titles and authors may be unfamiliar to younger students, while other books and authors may provide a review for older students. Teachers are encouraged to adapt each set of questions to the needs and abilities of his or her individual students.

Cast of Characters

Here is a list of some famous fictional people. In what novel would you find each of these characters?

1. Bob Cratchit
2. Mary Lennox
3. Becky Thatcher
4. Phillip Enright and Timothy
5. Mrs. Whatsit, Mrs. Which, and Mrs. Who
6. Aunt Sponge and Aunt Spiker
7. Jem, Scout, and Atticus Finch
8. Laurie, Marmee, and Mr. Bhaer
9. Rebecca Rowena Randall and her aunts, Miranda and Jane Sawyer

10. Captain Nemo
11. Gene and Phineas, students at Devon School
12. Ponyboy, Sodapop, Dallas, and Two-Bit
13. Fagin and the Dodger
14. Fiver, Buckthorn, Hazel, and Bigwig
15. Natty Bumppo and Chingachgook

Villainous Villains

Name these classic literary villains.

1. the red-golden dragon with wings "like an immeasurable bat" in *The Hobbit* by J. R. R. Tolkien

2. the wicked queen in *The Lion, the Witch and the Wardrobe* by C. S. Lewis

3. the crocodile-fearing pirate who was captain of the *Jolly Roger*

4. the evil bilge rat with "ragged fur and curved, jagged teeth" in *Redwall* by Brian Jacques

5. the pirate Jim Hawkins faced in *Treasure Island* by Robert Louis Stevenson

6. the cruel overseer of slaves in *Uncle Tom's Cabin* by Harriet Beecher Stowe

7. the purely evil personality created by a scientist seeking to separate his good and evil natures

8. the clerk who nearly ruins Mr. Wickfield and embezzles Betsey Trotwood's fortune in *David Copperfield*

9. the war leader whose head was a skull with sweeping antlers in *The Book of Three* by Lloyd Alexander

10. the evil professor of mathematics who was the arch-enemy of detective Sherlock Holmes

Middle School Language Arts Challenge
© The Learning Works, Inc.

Who Said That?

Identify the speakers of the following literary lines, name the book or play in which each line appears, and identify the author.

1. "It's really a wonder that I haven't dropped all my ideals. . . . Yet I keep them, because in spite of everything, I still believe that people are really good at heart."

2. "After a moment, lying there in darkness, hearing the creak of the raft and feeling its motion, it all hit me. I was blind and we were lost at sea."

3. "My orders are that every single child in this country shall be rrrubbed out, sqvashed, sqvirted, and frrittered before I come here again in vun year's time! "

4. "What a curious feeling! I must be shutting up like a telescope!"

5. "You must take my place, Jo, and be everything to father and mother when I'm gone."

6. "Oh, yes; the game was to just find something about everything to be glad about—no matter what 'twas."

7. "Does a boy get a chance to whitewash a fence every day?"

8. "I have ample evidence that you are being dogged in London. . . . You did not know, Dr. Mortimer, that you were followed this morning from my house?"

9. "But, soft! what light through yonder window breaks? It is the east, and Juliet is the sun."

10. "I've been making some mistakes, and each mistake has helped to cure me of some great shortcoming. The affair of the amethyst brooch cured me of meddling with things that didn't belong to me. . . . Dyeing my hair cured me of vanity."

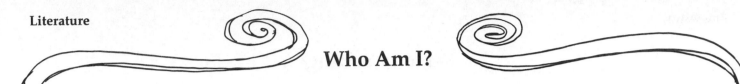

Who Am I?

Name the following literary characters, the book in which each appears, and the author of the book.

1. They say I was born in a dump. They say I kept an eight-inch cockroach on a leash and that rats kept guard over me while I slept. I'm allergic to pizza, and I am known for hitting the world's first home run on a fastfrog pitch. Who am I?

2. I moved from China to Brooklyn, where I learned to love baseball. Because of the generosity of my friend Emily, I was the one who presented the key to our school to Jackie Robinson! Who am I?

3. I lived on an island, yet I feared the sea because it killed my mother. One day I set out to conquer my fears head-on. Who am I?

4. I like to sit on the top of a forty-foot pole and look out over my home on Sarah's Mountain and the steel mining town of Harenton. Who am I?

5. I got into trouble for humming during the national anthem at Harrison High School. Who am I?

Middle School Language Arts Challenge
© The Learning Works, Inc.

Famous Settings

What novel or stories took place in each of the following famous settings?

1. Misselthwaite Manor
2. the Island of Krakatoa
3. Number Seventeen Cherry-Tree Lane
4. a tourist camp outside the town of Centerburg
5. the Metropolitan Museum of Art in New York City
6. the woods around Treegap
7. aboard the ship *The Seahawk*
8. a former Underground Railroad station in Ohio
9. a baseball diamond in a cornfield
10. aboard the slave ship *The Moonlight*
11. the palace of the Sultan Shahriar
12. a cave overlooking Lake Waccabuc during the Revolutionary War
13. 221B Baker Street
14. Tara
15. Thornfield Hall

Literary Geography

In what country or U. S. state do the following books take place?

1. *The Incredible Journey* by Sheila Burnford
2. *The Land I Lost* by Quang Nhuong Nhuong
3. *The Pushcart War* by Jean Merrill
4. *Roll of Thunder, Hear My Cry* by Mildred Taylor
5. *Anne of Green Gables* by L. M. Montgomery
6. *Heidi* by Johanna Spyri
7. *Julie of the Wolves* by Jean Craighead George
8. *Sadako and the Thousand Paper Cranes* by Eleanor Coerr
9. *Caddie Woodlawn* by Carol Ryrie Brink
10. *Anne Frank: The Diary of a Young Girl* by Anne Frank
11. *The Good Master* by Kate Seredy
12. *Wise Child* by Monica Furlong
13. *The Pearl* by John Steinbeck
14. *Cry, the Beloved Country* by Alan Paton
15. *Yung Fu of the Upper Yangtze* by Elizabeth Foreman Lewis

Middle School Language Arts Challenge
© The Learning Works, Inc.

Throughout History

Historical fiction uses a time period in the past as its setting. Name each of these books of historical fiction. Who wrote each one?

1. Set in southern Illinois during the Civil War, this is the story of Jethro Creighton, a boy who must run the family farm while his brothers are at war.

2. Thirteen-year-old Jonathan spends twenty-four hours as a soldier in the Revolutionary War and experiences the horrors of war.

3. This is the story of two friends, Annemarie Johansen and Ellen Rosen, and of how the Danes managed to smuggle nearly 7,000 Jews to Sweden so they would escape Nazi capture.

4. Thirteen-year-old Jessie Bollier witnesses the horrors of the slave trade while serving on a slave ship in 1840.

5. Set in Boston, this tale concerns a young silversmith who becomes involved in historic events on the eve of the Revolutionary War.

6. A young girl is stranded for eighteen years on an island off the coast of California in the 1800s.

7. Twelve-year-old Jack and Praiseworthy, the family butler, stow away on a ship sailing from Boston to California during the height of the gold rush.

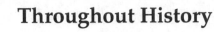

Throughout History

(continued)

8. This is the story of Sacajawea's best friend, who escaped after the girls were captured and taken from their Shoshoni tribe.

9. This story of a young Chinese boy's life in San Francisco in the early 1900s includes a description of the San Francisco earthquake.

10. Thirteen-year-old Catherine Cabot Hall helps a slave and thus defies the laws of the time.

11. A young boy's tales portray life in thirteenth century England as he searches for his minstrel father, Roger Quatermayne, and his dog, Nick.

12. A young boy becomes an apprentice in the Hanaza puppet theater in eighteenth-century Japan.

13. Set during the Depression, this book tells of the Logan family and their struggles against poverty and racial bigotry.

14. This is the account of a Japanese-American family's experiences in a California internment camp during World War II.

15. Set in Scotland during the 1740s, this book relates how young David Balfour encounters danger and adventure.

Middle School Language Arts Challenge
© The Learning Works, Inc.

Memorable Leads

Name the books that begin with each of the following opening lines:

1. There are dragons in the twins' vegetable garden.

2. All children, except one, grow up.

3. Brian Robeson stared out the window of the small plane at the endless green northern wilderness below.

4. You don't know about me without you have read a book by the name of *The Adventures of Tom Sawyer*, but that ain't no matter.

5. Miyax pushed back the hood of her sealskin parka and looked at the Arctic sun.

Memorable Leads

(continued)

6. Matthias cut a comical little figure as he wobbled his way along the cloisters, with his large sandals flip-flopping and his tail peeping from beneath the baggy folds of an oversized novice's habit.

7. This journey took place in a part of Canada which lies in the northwestern part of the great sprawling province of Ontario.

8. I, Catherine Cabot Hall, aged 13 years, 6 months, 29 days, of Meredith in the State of New-Hampshire, do begin this book.

9. Once there were three patients who met in the hospital and decided to live together.

10. To the red country and part of the gray country of Oklahoma, the last rains came gently, and they did not cut the scarred earth.

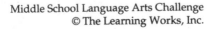

Middle School Language Arts Challenge
© The Learning Works, Inc.

Name That Author

Name the authors of the following books:

1. *The Yearling*
2. *Roll of Thunder, Hear My Cry*
3. *Rebecca of Sunnybrook Farm*
4. *Mrs. Frisby and the Rats of NIMH*
5. *Bambi*
6. *The Martian Chronicles*
7. *Hans Brinker or The Silver Skates*
8. *Scorpions*
9. *A Tree Grows in Brooklyn*
10. *Kidnapped*
11. *The Chocolate War*
12. *The Hero and the Crown*
13. *The Ring of Endless Light*
14. *Come Sing, Jimmy Jo*
15. *The Chosen*
16. *Ramona*

Literary Aliases

Sometimes authors invent names which they use when they write their books. These invented names—also called *noms de plume*, pseudonyms, or "pen" names—are often more familiar to readers than an author's real name. Under what *nom de plume* did each of the following authors write?

1. Samuel Langhorne Clemens
2. William Sydney Porter, the author of short stories such as "The Gift of the Magi"
3. Theodor Geisel
4. Reverend Charles Lutwidge Dodson
5. David Cornwell, the author of espionage novels
6. Eric Blair, the author of *1984*

Occasionally, authors use their given names to write most of their works but adopt "pen" names for other books or papers. What authors occasionally used these "pen" names?

7. Mary Westmacott, when she wrote romantic fiction instead of mysteries
8. Boz, better known as the author of *Bleak House* and *Oliver Twist*
9. Richard Saunders, of *Poor Richard's Almanack* fame
10. Diedrich Knickerbocker, better known as the author of "The Legend of Sleepy Hollow"

Middle School Language Arts Challenge
© The Learning Works, Inc.

Series of Series

Who wrote these famous literary series?

1. the Prydain Cycle
2. the Narnia series
3. Ramona books
4. Dragonriders of Pern
5. Black Stallion books
6. the Orphan Train Quartet
7. Oz books
8. Jane Marple mysteries

9. Hercule Poirot mysteries
10. Sherlock Holmes mysteries
11. The Lord of the Rings
12. The Dark Is Rising sequence
13. the Tripods Trilogy
14. Leatherstocking Tales
15. the Foundation series

Animals in Literature

Name these famous animals of literature. In what book did each appear, and who was the author?

1. "some" pig
2. the lead dog in the Iditarod team who had "too much wolf in him"
3. the hedgehog and the tortoise who tricked Painted Jaguar
4. the wolf-cub that bared its teeth to Gray Beaver
5. the character inspired by Edward Bear, a teddy bear owned by the author's son, Christopher
6. the two pigs who ran a farm with the motto "all animals are equal, but some animals are more equal than others"
7. a cat who could disappear, leaving only an enormous grin hanging in the air
8. the horse that won the Grand National steeplechase
9. the big, ugly dog whose name came from both his color and the sound he made
10. the pair of coon hounds bought by a ten-year-old boy growing up in the Ozark Mountains

Middle School Language Arts Challenge
© The Learning Works, Inc.

Animal Titles

Complete these titles with the missing animal name.

1. *The* _____, *the Witch and the Wardrobe* by C. S. Lewis
2. *Island of the Blue* _____ by Scott O'Dell
3. *A Day No* _____ *Would Die* by Robert Newton Peck
4. *Summer of the* _____ by Wilson Rawls
5. *Julie of the* _____ by Jean Craighead George
6. *The* _____ *Ate My Gymsuit* by Paula Danziger
7. *The Summer of the* _____ by Betsy Byars
8. *Incident at* _____ *'s Hill* by Allan W. Eckert
9. *To Kill a* _____ by Harper Lee
10. *Rumble* _____ by S. E. Hinton

Book Bouquets

Complete these titles with the name of the missing flower or plant word.

1. *Blue-Eyed* _____ by Cynthia Rylant

2. _____ *in Bloom* by Louisa May Alcott

3. *The Wind in the* _____ by Kenneth Grahame

4. *The December* _____ by Leon Garfield

5. *A* _____ *Grows in Brooklyn* by Betty Smith

6. *The Education of Little* _____ by Forrest Carter

7. *A View from the* _____ by Willo Davis Roberts

8. *The Sign of the* _____ by Katherine Paterson

9. *The Singing* _____ by Kate Seredy

10. *Anne of Windy* _____ by L. M. Montgomery

11. *Cold Sassy* _____ by Olive Ann Burns

12. _____ *Wine* by Ray Bradbury

13. _____ *for Algernon* by Daniel Keyes

14. *Where the* _____ *Bloom* by Vera and Bill Cleaver

15. *Tom's Midnight* _____ by Philippa Pearce

Middle School Language Arts Challenge
© The Learning Works, Inc.

Devouring a Good Book

Complete these titles with the missing food word.

1. _____ *Girl* by Lois Lenski
2. *About the B'nai* _____ by E. L. Konigsburg
3. *James and the Giant* _____ by Roald Dahl
4. _____ *Days and* _____ *Nights* by Gary Paulsen
5. *Fried Green* _____ *at the Whistle Stop Cafe* by Fannie Flagg
6. *The* _____ *War* by Robert Cormier
7. *The Wonderful Story of Henry* _____ by Roald Dahl
8. *Hello, My Name is* _____ by Jamie Gilson
9. _____ *John* by Joseph Krumgold
10. *Five Little* _____ *and How They Grew* by Margaret Sidney
11. *The Tattooed* _____ by Ellen Raskin
12. *The Animal, the* _____ *, and John D. Jones* by Betsy Byars
13. *The* _____ *Pig* by Nina Bawden
14. *The* _____ *of Wrath* by John Steinbeck
15. _____ *Blue* by Vera Cleaver

Colorful Literature

Name the authors of these "colorful" books.

1. *The Witch of Blackbird Pond*
2. *Redwall*
3. *A Solitary Blue*
4. *Black Star, Bright Dawn*
5. *The Red Pony*
6. *Pinky Pye*
7. *Anne of Green Gables*
8. *The Black Stallion*

9. *Island of the Blue Dolphins*
10. *The White Mountains*
11. *Big Red*
12. *The Children of Green Knowe*
13. *The Grey King*
14. *Where the Red Fern Grows*
15. *Green Grass of Wyoming*

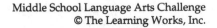

25

Poetic Quotes

Name the poet who wrote each of the following poems.

1. These woods are lovely, dark and deep,
   But I have promises to keep,
   And miles to go before I sleep . . .

2. There is no frigate like a book
   To take us lands away

3. The fog comes
   on little cat feet.

4. I will not play at tug o' war,
   I'd rather play at hug o' war . . .

5. Under the spreading chestnut tree
   The village smithy stands.

6. But there is no joy in Mudville—
   Mighty Casey has struck out.

7. I've known rivers:
   I've known rivers ancient as the world
   and older than
   the flow of human blood in human veins.

Who was the first poet to particpate in a presidential inauguration?

The Extraordinary Newbery

Look at the list of Newbery Award-winning books and their authors. Match each book with its author by writing the correct letter in the blank.

_____	1. *Hitty, Her First Hundred Years*	A.	Betsy Byars
_____	2. *Jacob Have I Loved*	B.	Eleanor Estes
_____	3. *The Summer of the Swans*	C.	Madeleine L'Engle
_____	4. *The Giver*	D.	Joseph Krumgold
_____	5. *The Slave Dancer*	E.	Rachel Field
_____	6. *Ginger Pye*	F.	Lois Lowry
_____	7. *Onion John*	G.	Katherine Paterson
_____	8. *A Wrinkle in Time*	H.	Carol Ryrie Brink
_____	9. *Caddie Woodlawn*	I.	Armstrong Sperry
_____	10. *Call It Courage*	J.	Paula Fox

Middle School Language Arts Challenge
© The Learning Works, Inc.

More Newbery

Look at the list of Newbery Award-winning books and their authors. Match each book with its author by writing the correct letter in the blank.

_____ 1. *Adam of the Road*   A. Eric P. Kelly

_____ 2. *Dear Mr. Henshaw*   B. Jean Craighead George

_____ 3. *Julie of the Wolves*   C. Elizabeth Borton de Trevino

_____ 4. *Shiloh*   D. Elizabeth Janet Gray

_____ 5. *The Westing Game*   E. Mildred Taylor

_____ 6. *The Trumpeter of Krakow*   F. Hugh Lofting

_____ 7. *I, Juan de Pareja*   G. Phyllis Reynolds Naylor

_____ 8. *Roll of Thunder, Hear My Cry*   H. Beverly Cleary

_____ 9. *The Voyages of Dr. Dolittle*   I. Cynthia Voigt

_____ 10. *Dicey's Song*   J. Ellen Raskin

How many other Newbery Award-winning books can you name? Write their titles and authors. Name the book that won the first Newbery Award in 1922.

Literary Trivia

1. What author of classic novels was also one of the first Canadian women journalists?

2. What famous author of "Hiawatha" lost his wife when her clothes caught fire? (He was unable to attend her funeral—which took place on their wedding anniversary—because of burns he suffered trying to save her.)

3. The man who wrote *Of Mice and Men* feared winning the Nobel Prize because he believed he would never write again if he won it. (And, in fact, he published no new works between 1962, when he won the Nobel Prize, and his death in 1968.)

4. This author began his first novel, *The Black Stallion*, when he was still in high school.

5. What fictional character's full name was Pippilotta Delicatessa Windowshade MacKrelmint Efrain's Daughter?

6. What author had her manuscript for *A Wrinkle in Time* rejected by twenty-six publishers in two years before it was accepted for publication?

7. Her first book, *Flower Fables* (1854), was a collection of tales written for Ralph Waldo Emerson's daughter.

Middle School Language Arts Challenge
© The Learning Works, Inc.

Literary Trivia
(continued)

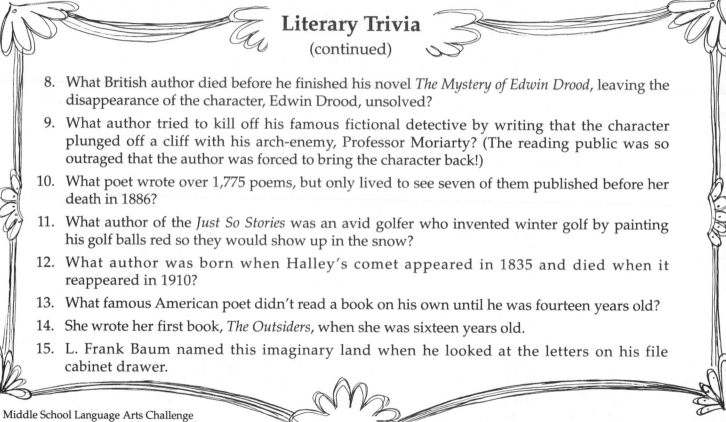

8. What British author died before he finished his novel *The Mystery of Edwin Drood*, leaving the disappearance of the character, Edwin Drood, unsolved?

9. What author tried to kill off his famous fictional detective by writing that the character plunged off a cliff with his arch-enemy, Professor Moriarty? (The reading public was so outraged that the author was forced to bring the character back!)

10. What poet wrote over 1,775 poems, but only lived to see seven of them published before her death in 1886?

11. What author of the *Just So Stories* was an avid golfer who invented winter golf by painting his golf balls red so they would show up in the snow?

12. What author was born when Halley's comet appeared in 1835 and died when it reappeared in 1910?

13. What famous American poet didn't read a book on his own until he was fourteen years old?

14. She wrote her first book, *The Outsiders*, when she was sixteen years old.

15. L. Frank Baum named this imaginary land when he looked at the letters on his file cabinet drawer.

Authors with Challenges

Name these authors who faced special challenges in their lives.

1. This Nobel Prize-winning author of *For Whom the Bell Tolls* and *The Old Man and the Sea* lived with diabetes.

2. This author of *A Child's Garden of Verses* battled lung disease most of his life.

3. A writer of imaginative fairy tales, this author had dyslexia and had his publishers correct his many spelling errors.

4. This author of *A Connecticut Yankee in King Arthur's Court* suffered from insomnia.

5. The author of *Pickwick Papers*, this famous novelist lived on his own at the age of twelve after his family was sent to debtors' prison.

6. These famous British literary sisters left boarding school after their two older sisters, who also attended the school, died of tuberculosis.

7. This author of *Brave New World* wanted to become a doctor, but he gave up his plans at age sixteen when an eye disease nearly blinded him. (He still managed to write an 80,000 word novel—never published—by the time he was seventeen years old!)

8. This author of *Mine for Keeps* has only partial sight and has used a special talking computer to write.

Middle School Language Arts Challenge
© The Learning Works, Inc.

Odd Jobs

Many authors held unusual jobs or pursued non-literary interests at one time or another in their lives. Match these authors with their various jobs or interests.

_____	1. a railway hobo, an oyster pirate, and a coal stoker	A. Sid Fleischman
_____	2. a lawyer and an airline reservations clerk	B. Harper Lee
_____	3. an ambulance driver for the French army during World War I	C. Charles Dickens
_____	4. a bank clerk who was imprisoned for embezzling funds	D. Gary Paulsen
_____	5. a chemistry teacher who blew up the laboratory sink	E. Jack London
_____	6. a professional magician	F. John Steinbeck
_____	7. a trapper, a singer, and a participant in the Iditarod	G. Enid Bagnold
_____	8. a boot polish factory worker	H. Louisa May Alcott
_____	9. a boxer, an ambulance driver, and a reporter	I. L. Frank Baum
_____	10. the editor of a magazine for store window decorators	J. O. Henry
_____	11. a bricklayer for Madison Square Gardens	K. Ernest Hemingway
_____	12. a hospital nurse who cared for the wounded after the Battle of Fredericksburg	L. E. L. Konigsberg

Creative Writing

Ingenious Inventions

Select a title from the list below and design an invention with that name. In 100 words or less, describe what your invention looks like and how it works. Tell a story of how and why you invented it. Draw a picture of your invention and label its parts.

Homework Helper	Super Saver
Bodacious Bedmaker	Fantastic Flyer
Allowance Allocator	Refrigerator Raider
Weedin' Wizard	Dandy Snack Dispenser
Chore-Aid	Phenomenal Phone
Awesome Alarm Clock	The Better Bleacher

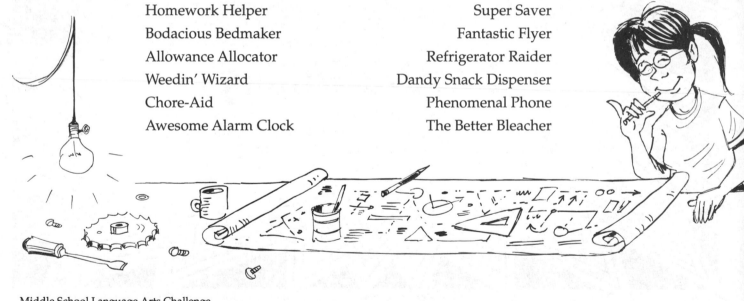

Creative Writing

Four-By-Four Stories

Pick any four items from the first column and any four characters from the second column. Write a story that contains all of the items and characters you have selected.

a basketball trophy	Marcia, who loves cats
an endangered fish	Brian, who plays practical jokes
a pink skateboard	Carl, who is afraid of the dark
chalk dust	Ms. Santos, a forgetful math teacher
a blackout	Ms. Jefferson, the soccer coach
a gopher	Zoe, who has a photographic memory
tire tracks	Mr. Chu, the librarian
a bag of jelly beans	Dina, a mischievous toddler
a ripped feather pillow	Jo, owner of Hangin' Around Hang Gliding
a bent baseball card	Dr. Gerard, the dentist
spilled sugar	Angela, who is extremely shy
a smelly sock	Pedro, who can read minds
a missed goal	Dr. Long, a nearsighted pediatrician
a mutant vegetable	Frank, owner of Tower of Pizza restaurant
the winning ticket	Mr. Stanley, who has seven children
a bungee cord	Ms. Fox, a mother who oversleeps
a bedraggled puppy	Chester, who is homeless

Middle School Language Arts Challenge
© The Learning Works, Inc.

Under the Microscope

Pick one of the following items and write three paragraphs on how it might be used if it were much smaller. For example, a river raft could be used as a bathtub soap dish. If you prefer, think of your own item to miniaturize.

lawn mower	pizza oven
chain link fence	podium
cowboy boot	saddle
doctor's stethoscope	saw
dog house	skyscraper
hot air balloon	football goal post

Bigger Than Life

Pick one of the following items and write three paragraphs on how it might be used if it were much larger in size. For example, an oversized fork could be used to rake leaves. If you prefer, think of your own item to enlarge.

picture frame	soccer net
fly swatter	spoon
harmonica	steering wheel
paint brush	top hat
piece of macaroni	umbrella
popsicle stick	zipper

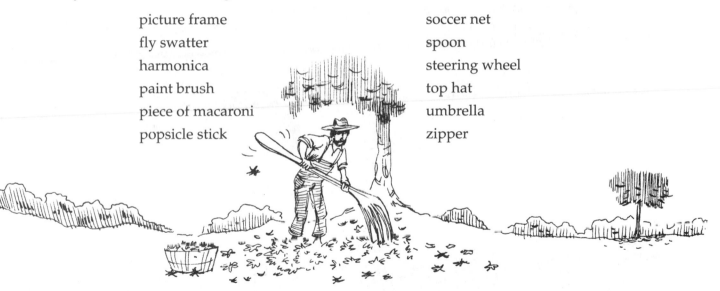

37

The Turning Point

Think of a critical moment in history and write a story about how you alter the course of events by your actions. For example, you could describe how you cause John F. Kennedy's motorcade to take an alternate route, thereby foiling the assassination. Make your story realistic by including historical facts and people.

See Middle-Earth!

Write a travel brochure for a fictional place that has formed the setting for a book or story you have read. Be sure to point out several reasons to visit this place and describe its most appealing sights and attractions. Include drawings of places of interest. Tell how travelers might get there and what they should bring when they visit.

Examples of fictional places:

The Island of Krakatoa from *The Twenty-One Balloons*

Neverland, where Peter Pan lives

Middle-Earth, as created in books by J. R. R. Tolkien

Middle School Language Arts Challenge
© The Learning Works, Inc.

Nice to Know You

What might happen if you could meet a character from a novel, story, poem, or play you have read? For example, what if Tom Sawyer were a new student in your class? What if Captain Hook were your teacher?

Pick a fictional character to place somewhere in your life—at school, at home, on your basketball team, etc. Describe how you and the character would get along, how things might be different because of the character's presence, and how the character might perceive things that you find commonplace, such as television, computers, cars, etc.

Difficult Dilemmas

Some of the most effective literature puts the main character in the midst of a dilemma that forces him or her to make difficult choices. How the character handles the dilemma tells readers a lot.

Write a short story in which the main character faces a difficult dilemma.

Perhaps your character must decide whether or not to

take action that violates his or her values
betray a friendship or a family member
use power or deceit to accomplish a goal
do "the right thing" when doing so may create another problem

Use the character's own actions, words, or thoughts to show how your character handles the dilemma. You can also use the way other characters speak to, think about, or treat the main character.

Middle School Language Arts Challenge
© The Learning Works, Inc.

Snapshot Impressions

Sometimes the inspiration for a story comes from an everyday event or an impression of an ordinary occurrence. Look around you and take mental pictures of the things you notice. Use one of these "snapshots" in a short story you write.

Examples:
- a discarded receipt lying against the schoolyard fence
- a girl angrily slamming a car door
- the faded scar on a neighbor's arm
- a rusty toy dump truck left in a park
- someone else's photo mixed in with the vacation photos you just had developed
- an "urgent" telephone message to call Pronto Pizza
- a woman anxiously searching through her purse
- a note dropping, unnoticed, from a student's book

Foreshadowing

Authors often use **foreshadowing**, mentioning at an earlier point in the story something that hints at or sets the stage for an event that will come later in the story. Foreshadowing helps to build suspense and heighten the reader's interest. Write a story in which you use foreshadowing. Use one of the ideas listed below, or create your own.

a sudden stomach cramp

a travel poster in a store window

sunscreen left on the kitchen counter

a four-leaf clover

a tall woman in a red hat at the back of a crowd

"I think I could win if I just had the courage to try."

"I never learned how to swim."

43

In Other Words

Could you describe brushing your teeth without using the words *tooth* or *brush*? You might say you were cleaning your pearly-whites with a long-handled, soft-bristled dental scrubbing utensil!

Choose one of the tasks below and write a one-page description without using any of the words listed after the task. Use your imagination—and a thesaurus—to help you.

roasting a marshmallow   *roast, marshmallow, fire, stick*

brushing your hair   *hair, brush, stroke*

blowing out birthday candles   *birthday, cake, candles, flame*

bathing a dog   *dog, bath, water, soap*

canoeing   *canoe, oar, water, river*

Journalism and
Journal Writing

Extra! Extra!

London, New York, and Los Angeles all have newpapers called *The Times*. Another popular name for a newspaper is *The News*—Detroit, Buffalo, and Dayton all have newspapers with this name. Write the letter for the correct city in the blank next to the newspaper that is published there.

_____	1. The Times-Picayune	A.	Chicago
_____	2. The Chronicle	B.	Atlanta
_____	3. The Inquirer	C.	New Orleans
_____	4. The Enquirer	D.	Cincinnati
_____	5. The Tribune	E.	Hartford
_____	6. The Observer	F.	San Francisco
_____	7. The Globe	G.	Indianapolis
_____	8. The Courant	H.	Charlotte
_____	9. The Star	I.	Philadelphia
_____	10. The Constitution	J.	Boston

What other major metropolitan newspapers can you name? Write their names and the cities where they are published.

By-Lines by You

Every news story should include information that answers the questions *Who, What, Where, When, Why,* and *How.* Pick one of the following scenarios and write a 100-word story that answers those questions and incorporates these facts:

Your school basketball team scored an upset victory over its biggest rival.

Scientists have discovered that talking on the telephone causes memory loss in teens.

Someone in your community just won the Nobel Peace Prize.

Make your story interesting by inventing quotes and facts to include. Then write an attention-grabbing headline for your story—one that takes up exactly 50 spaces. Count each letter, punctuation mark, and space between words as one space. For example, *Kids Discover Ancient Treasures in School Basement* is exactly 50 spaces.

WHO? WHAT? WHEN? WHERE? WHY? HOW?

Middle School Language Arts Challenge
© The Learning Works, Inc.

A Pivotal Moment

Describe a pivotal moment or event in your life—other than your birth—that made an impact on who you are or what has happened to you since.

Other than your parents, is there a person who has been especially important in your life? Describe this person and how he or she has influenced you or changed your life.

Object Lesson

Imagine that every object you owned was destroyed. Think about the following questions and then write one or two paragraphs describing how you think you would feel. Try to answer all the questions.

What objects do you think you could do without?

What kinds of things do you think you would miss most?

Are your possessions important to you? Why or why not?

If you could have saved one thing from being destroyed, what would it have been? Why is this item so important to you?

Middle School Language Arts Challenge
© The Learning Works, Inc.

Portrait of a Writer

If you hired someone to paint your portrait, what would you expect the artist to show about you in the painting? What would you wear? What objects or other people, if any, would you include in your portrait?

Write a description of your portrait and tell what it shows about you as a person.

Dinner at My House

If you could invite one person from history or literature to dinner at your house, who would it be? Why would you invite that person? If you could add three more historical or literary figures to your dinner, who would they be? Why did you choose them? How would they get along? Would they be interested in talking to one another? What would they like to know? What food would you serve your guests?

Write a description, dialogue, or short play showing how your guests interact at dinner. If you can, work into your writing a brief explanation of why you invited each guest.

Middle School Language Arts Challenge
© The Learning Works, Inc.

Most-ly Me

Think about some of the "superlative" moments in your life.

- most embarrassing
- most awkward
- most frightening
- most frustrating
- most ashamed
- most important

- happiest
- proudest
- angriest
- saddest
- quietest
- funniest

Choose three "superlative" moments to write about, or think of your own superlatives to add to the list and write about them instead.

Punctuation, Grammar, and Usage

Pesky Apostrophes

Apostrophes are used in contractions (can't, you've, it's), in possessive nouns (the Smiths' house, James's book, the child's mother), in plurals of letters (dot your *i*'s), and in words referred to as words (replace the *said*'s in your writing). In the paragraph below, insert apostrophes where they are needed.

Its surprising to me that kids today dont read more of Mark Twains novels. After youve read his tales of the Mississippi, youll find yourself laughing at all of his characters wild adventures. Maybe one of the problems kids have with Twains books is deciding how many *ps*, *is*, and *ss* to put in all those *Mississippis* they have to write in their reports. Theres a way around that, though, if youre creative. In Jamals report on *The Adventures of Huckleberry Finn*, Jamal counted four *is*, four *ss*, and two *ps* each time he used the word *Mississippi*. Claryces solution was to refer to "that big, muddy river," avoiding the problem altogether!

Periods and Commas

In the paragraph below, insert commas and periods in their proper places. Be sure to change lower case letters to upper case, if necessary.

Although Kevin was normally on time today he was going to be late first his alarm didn't go off next the shower was out of hot water finally as he sat down to breakfast he spilled his cereal on the floor he went to the garage to get a broom and the back door closed behind him he was locked out and the only way into the house was through the dog door as he crawled through the tiny door his dog Pavlov licked Kevin's face neck and hands Kevin was beginning to think this awful frustrating morning would never end!

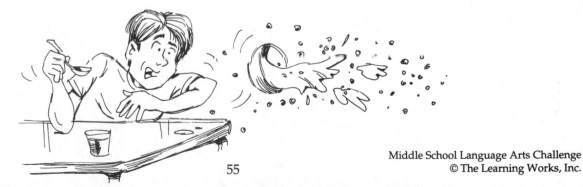

Middle School Language Arts Challenge
© The Learning Works, Inc.

A Plethora of Plurals

Many plurals are formed simply by adding the letter *s* to the end of the word. However, many plurals are formed in other ways. What are the plural forms of the following words?

1. ox
2. datum
3. passerby
4. potato
5. comedy

6. alumnus
7. alumna
8. die (a cube)
9. cactus
10. mother-in-law

11. moose
12. louse
13. crisis
14. half
15. alga

A Capital Idea

In the following paragraph, find the errors in capitalization. Draw three lines under each letter that should be capitalized, but isn't; draw a slash through each letter that is capitalized incorrectly.

For example: my family and i went to florida last Summer.

When i went to Washington, d.c., with my family over Spring Break, I saw many interesting sights. in may, the Cherry Blossoms are in bloom, and i took lots of pictures with my new Pocket-sized Camera. My favorite Monument was the Jefferson memorial, although my Sister liked the capitol best. we even met our senator, lotta Votz, who arranged a tour of the white House for us. We did not, however, meet president Partisan, who was touring the far East with the Secretary of state.

Middle School Language Arts Challenge
© The Learning Works, Inc.

Misplaced Modifiers

A **modifier** is a word or phrase that describes another word or phrase. The modifier should be close to whatever it modifies. When it isn't, the sentence can be confusing—or even silly.

Correct the misplaced modifiers in the sentences below by writing the sentences correctly.

1. President Lincoln wrote the Gettysburg Address while he was traveling on the back of an envelope.
2. Jessica broke her leg while she was skiing in three places.
3. Rosie pitched baseballs to her dog, who was trying out for the varsity team.
4. The orthodontist with a sharp twist adjusted Katherine's braces.
5. Dropping from the sky, I caught the ball.

Write ten sentences of your own that have misplaced modifiers.

They're, Their, There

The English language is filled with words that sound or look alike. The following sentences use some tricky and easily confused words. Underline the correct choice. You may use the dictionary if you need help.

1. When Beth dropped her box of (stationary, stationery), (loose, lose) pens and papers scattered all over the floor.

2. Because Miranda and Cecil are (pour, poor) cooks, (it's, its) a good idea to have (dessert, desert) before (dinner, diner) at (their, they're, there) house.

3. The (mayor, mare) wants (your, you're) (advise, advice) on the proposed (site, sight, cite) for the (new, knew) (capitol, capital) building near the (maul, mall).

4. By the time we got (through, threw) the tunnel, the school bus was (already, all ready) (past, passed) the (toll, told) booth.

5. I did not (except, accept) the money, since doing so would have violated my (principals, principles) about taking (elicit, illicit) funds.

6. I'd rather (proceed, precede) along a (moral, morale) (coarse, course), of (coarse, course), (than, then) go against my (conscience, conscious).

7. The rain (would of, would have) had an (affect, effect) on the condition of the soccer field, (to, too, two).

Middle School Language Arts Challenge
© The Learning Works, Inc.

In Agreement

The subject and verb of every sentence must agree in number. For example, *the girl laughs* (singular) or *the girls laugh* (plural). There are times, however, when determining the proper agreement of the subject and verb can be tricky. Underline the correct verb in each of the following sentences.

1. Either Ms. Power or the coach (drive, drives) the bus to the games.
2. There (is, are) many ways to get to the stadium.
3. There (is, are), however, only one fast way to go.
4. The driver, as well as the kids on the team, (watch, watches) the road.
5. Everyone (yell, yells) when the driver misses the turn.
6. Despite many wrong turns, the team (arrive, arrives) on time.
7. Everyone (wait, waits) for the bus to stop before standing up.
8. Neither Margo nor Beth (was, were) ready to leave the bus.
9. The team (was, were) desperate to get to the field.
10. Each of the players (was, were) ready to leave without Margo and Beth.

Agreeable Pronouns

A **pronoun** is a word that is used in place of a noun. Underline the correct pronoun in each of the following sentences.

1. Each of the boys called (his, their) mother.
2. Taylor and (I, me) ordered asparagus with dinner.
3. Matthew kept the news to (hisself, himself).
4. Neither Alfredo nor David stood on (his, their) desk.
5. Pass the note to Kim and (I, me) when the teacher leaves the room.
6. Each girl takes (her, their) turn at bat.
7. James and Penny wrote the play (theirselves, themselves).
8. Each boy threw (his, their) paper in the trash.
9. When we went to the parking lot, my mother and (I, me) couldn't find the car.
10. (She, Her) and Mavis missed the bus again.
11. (Who, Whom) will you invite to the party?
12. (Who, Whom) is coming to the party?

Middle School Language Arts Challenge
© The Learning Works, Inc.

Regularly Irregular

Most verbs are **regular**, which means you add *d* or *ed* to make the past tense or the past participle. (*Today I skate. Yesterday I skated. I have skated many times this week.*) However, many verbs do not follow this rule. They are called **irregular verbs**. Some of the verbs in the following sentences are regular, while others are irregular. Write the correct form of each verb in the space provided.

1. Amy (know) _____ that Masumi had (**lend**) _____ her last dollar to Sara.

2. Chris, the star player, (**stride**) _____ into the room.

3. The energetic dancer (**spring**) _____ to her feet and (**swing**) _____ her arms wildly in the air.

4. While Tom's mother (**set**) _____ limits on his curfew, he (**wring**) _____ his handkerchief and (**weep**) _____ .

Regularly Irregular

(continued)

5. Marco (**freeze**) _____ and (**wish**) _____ he had
   (**flee**)_____ when he (**see**) _____ the school bully, who
   (**arise**)_____ from the front steps.

6. Tina (**lay**)_____ her head down and (**cling**) _____ to the
   railing above the cliff.

7. Fran (**creep**)_____ quietly toward the door and then (**burst**)
   _____ noisily into the kitchen.

8. As she (**slide**) _____ into third base, she (**swear**) _____
   she would practice sprinting tomorrow.

Middle School Language Arts Challenge
© The Learning Works, Inc.

Proofreader's Symbols

Symbol	Meaning	Example
ℓ	delete	New York, New York
∧	insert	New York, New York
#	insert space	New York, New York
⌒	delete space	New York, New York
≡	make upper case	new york, new york
/	make lower case	NEw York, NeW YOrk
∼	transpose letters	Nwe York, Nwe York
∼	transpose words	York New York New
⌄	insert comma	New York New York
⊙	insert period	We went to New York

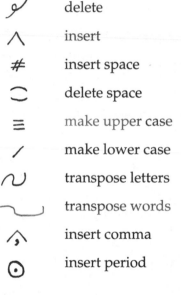

Proof It

Use proofreader's symbols to correct the following sentences.

1. pat threew theball from second to frist base to complEte the double ply for the tgiers.

2. wheen she retruned her to desk cAthy foundthe hmework shee Thought she lost had.

3. the principla of litle muontian shcoool Called mary, rosa, and t6odd tothe offiec for improtnat meeTnig.

4. scottts' mther beggged hmi To chnage the raido Statoin

5. tHe boy s lostthe socer g ame AT recesss .

Middle School Language Arts Challenge
© The Learning Works, Inc.

Sentence Diagram Models

A good way to show the relationship between parts of a sentence is to use a **diagram**, or a picture of its structure. Here are some examples of sentence diagrams.

My brother plays the kazoo.

Felicia and Alex are my favorite players.

Maria walked slowly to the door.

The girls danced wildly to the loud music.

Stan and Linda dined happily at Harry's house.

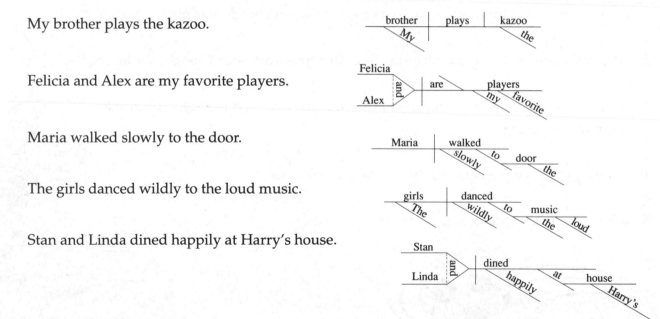

Dynamite Diagrams

On a separate sheet of paper, diagram the sentences below. Use a ruler to make your diagram outlines.

1. William played an exciting game of checkers.
2. Janelle ordered a small salad and a chocolate sundae.
3. Marco plays piano and flute.
4. The girls are excellent runners.
5. Beth and Javier brought Denise to the game.
6. The girls on our team are great athletes.
7. My dad stopped at the grocery store.
8. I can catch grapes in my mouth.
9. Camp food is very good.
10. My math teacher wrote six difficult problems on the board.

Middle School Language Arts Challenge
© The Learning Works, Inc.

Parts-of-Speech Stories

To the teacher: *Photocopy each "parts-of-speech" story for repeated use. Without reading the story out loud, call out the parts of speech that are written beneath the blank lines. Ask students to supply a word that is the correct part of speech. Write in one word per blank and then read the story aloud, using the students' suggested words.*

If necessary, explain the following definitions:

Present participle: a verb form that ends in *ing* and that modifies a noun or a pronoun; like a verb, it may have an object

Present infinitive: a form of a verb introduced by *to*

Superlative modifier: degree of comparison among more than two things, usually shown by the letters *est* or the word *most*

Parts-of-Speech Story I

Blanche White, director of the upcoming movie "Mystery of the Broken _____,"
(noun)

was in town looking for new talent. She needed a/an _____ girl to play Fifi,
(adjective)

the _____ detective, and a/an _____ boy to play Herman,
(adjective)   (adjective)

the _____ who had been accused of stealing _____ from
(noun)   (plural noun)

_____ . As Blanche walked _____ to the school office,
(noun)   (adverb)

she spotted _____ _____ on the playground with
(name of girl in class)(present participle)

her _____ friends. "_____!" Blanche shouted. "You are
(adjective)   (interjection)

perfect for Fifi! Have you ever _____ in a film before?"
(past tense regular verb)

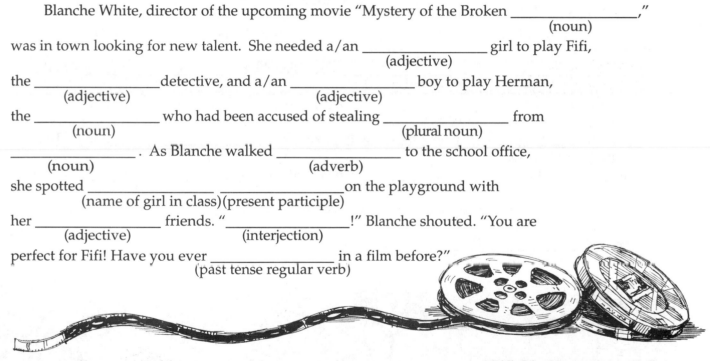

Middle School Language Arts Challenge
© The Learning Works, Inc.

Parts-of-Speech Story I

(continued)

"No, not since I was _____ years old," she replied. Just then,

(number)

_____ _____ by. Blanche ran _____ to the

(name of boy in class)   (past tense verb)   (adverb)

office, exclaiming _____ to the principal, "I want two of your students

(adverb)

_____ in my new film! I will make them _____ stars!" The

(present infinitive)   (adjective)

principal replied as _____ as he could, "I'm sorry, Blanche. These kids are not

(adverb)

free to go with you. We need them here for our school play, *The* _____*That*

(noun)

Terrorized _____."

(proper noun–place)

Parts-of-Speech Story II

Ms. Reina Terror, the _____ weightlifter of the decade, has announced a new
(superlative modifier)

exercise program for _____ middle school students. Her program will include
(adjective)

special exercises, like the _____ toe-touch, the _____ jog, and
(adjective)   (present participle)

the _____ arm stretch. Students will run _____ around the
(adjective)   (adverb)

track in an effort _____ their muscles. The obstacle course includes jumping
(present infinitive)

over _____, hanging from _____ , and _____
(plural noun)   (plural noun)   (present participle)

under _____ . _____ _____ and jumped for
(plural noun)   (name of someone in room)   (past tense verb)

_____ as soon as the program was announced.
(noun)

Middle School Language Arts Challenge
© The Learning Works, Inc.

Parts-of-Speech Story III

Have you heard about the _____ rock group? It is called "The
(superlative modifier)

_____ _____ Mashers," and it is the _____
(adjective)   (noun)   (superlative modifier)

group on the rock scene this year. The lead singer has _____ hair and
(adjective)

clothes and wears a/an_____ around his neck. The group's music sounds like a
(noun)

screechy_____ and has been compared to a/an _____
(noun)   (adjective)

_____ . After the group performs, the members of the group dine at local
(noun)

restaurants, where they enjoy delicious _____ and healthy _____ .
(plural noun)   (plural noun)

Then they board their luxurious _____ , and they're off to their next
(noun, form of transportation)

_____ concert.
(adjective)

Vocabulary

Artistic Vocabulary

Select six words from the list below. Look the words up in the dictionary if you do not know what they mean.

Make a drawing that shows the meaning of each word you picked. Write the word's origin, pronunciation, and definition on the back of your drawing.

atelier	kitsch	topiary
bon vivant	lanate	unguinous
congenial	mansuetude	vagarious
dressage	natatorium	whelp
epaulet	oppidan	xenophobia
fuliginous	panjandrum	yawl
girandole	quotidian	zephyr
hibernaculum	raconteur	
impecunious	skirl	

Worldly Word Origins

Many English words are borrowed from other languages or have their origins in another language. Write the correct letter to match the words below to their definitions in their original languages.

_____	1. klutz
_____	2. espresso
_____	3. gusto
_____	4. gauche
_____	5. alibi
_____	6. lilac
_____	7. gumbo
_____	8. hibachi
_____	9. orangutan
_____	10. yam
_____	11. pajamas
_____	12. succotash
_____	13. dachsund
_____	14. dinosaur
_____	15. dandelion

A. Arabic: bluish in color
B. German: badger dog
C. Malay: man of the woods
D. Yiddish: clumsy person
E. Hindu: leg garment
F. Italian: dark coffee
G. Spanish: pleasure
H. Senegalese: to eat
I.   Greek: terrible lizard
J.   French: left
K. Algonquin: something broken into pieces
L. Bantu: okra
M. Japanese: fire pot
N. Latin: at another place
O. French: lion's tooth

Middle School Language Arts Challenge
© The Learning Works, Inc.

Namesakes

Words are often based on people's names. Write the word that has its origin in each of the following proper names. Then do some research and write a short paragraph about at least three of these people whose names were turned into words.

1. Joseph Guillotin
2. Louis Pasteur
3. Thomas Bowdler
4. Joel R. Poinsett
5. Nicholas Chauvin

6. Jean Nicot
7. Antoine Joseph Sax
8. Franz Anton Mesmer
9. Levi Strauss
10. Major General Ambrose E. Burnsides

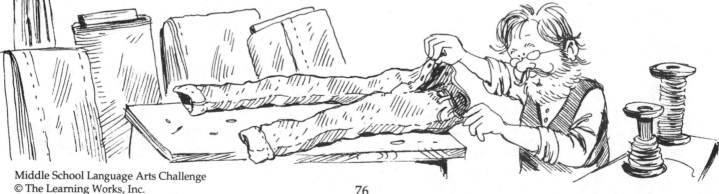

Occupations

Match the occupation in the first column with its description in the second column by writing the correct letter in each blank.

_____ 1. agronomist

_____ 2. bailiff

_____ 3. cartographer

_____ 4. endocrinologist

_____ 5. etymologist

_____ 6. graphologist

_____ 7. herpetologist

_____ 8. hydrologist

_____ 9. phrenologist

_____ 10. stevedore

A. one who studies handwriting

B. one who studies word origins and histories

C. a mapmaker

D. one who studies soil management

E. a scientist who studies water

F. a physician specializing in diseases of the glands

G. a zoologist specializing in reptiles and amphibians

H. an officer of the court

I. one who studies the skull

J. one who loads and unloads the cargo of a ship in port

Middle School Language Arts Challenge
© The Learning Works, Inc.

The Hobbyist

What do you like to do in your spare time? Match the word in the first column with the corresponding hobby in the second column by writing the correct letter in each blank.

_____ 1. numismatics

_____ 2. spelunking

_____ 3. philately

_____ 4. alpinism

_____ 5. tatting

_____ 6. whittling

_____ 7. funambulism

_____ 8. crocheting

_____ 9. oology

_____ 10. genealogy

A. mountain climbing

B. lace making

C. cave exploring

D. paring wood into shapes

E. tightrope walking

F. stamp collecting

G. study of families and ancestors

H. the study or collection of birds' eggs

I. coin collecting

J. interlocking looped stitches into sweaters, blankets, etc.

Don't ~~Mispell~~ Misspell It

The National Spelling Bee is held annually in Washington, D.C. Below are some of the winning words in this competition. See how many of them you can spell. Then look up each word in the dictionary, write its definition, and use it in a sentence.

1. abalone
2. antipyretic
3. chihuahua
4. croissant
5. elegiacal
6. fibranne
7. hydrophyte
8. incisor
9. kamikaze
10. luge
11. lyceum

12. milieu
13. narcolepsy
14. odontalgia
15. onerous
16. propylaeum
17. psoriasis
18. Purim
19. sarcophagus
20. shalloon
21. spoliator
22. staphylococci

Middle School Language Arts Challenge
© The Learning Works, Inc.

Don't Myth Out

Many English words come from Greek or Roman mythology. On the following page, match the definitions in the first column to the words in the second column by writing the correct letters in the blanks provided.

Then look in the word box below to find the mythological figure whose name is the origin of the word given. Write the name of the mythological character on the line next to the word on which it is based.

Word Box	
Atlas	Pan
Ceres	Prometheus
Hercules	Tantalus
Mars	the Titans
Narcissus	Vulcan

Don't Myth Out

(continued)

_____ 1. self-centered

_____ 2. a collection of maps

_____ 3. warlike

_____ 4. related to grain

_____ 5. daringly original

_____ 6. a sudden, overpowering fright

_____ 7. mockingly or enticingly out of reach

_____ 8. colossal or gigantic

_____ 9. to treat a synthetic material
to give it properties such
as elasticity, strength, or stability

_____ 10. of extraordinary power or difficulty

A. cereal _____

B. panic _____

C. narcissistic _____

D. vulcanize _____

E. martial _____

F. herculean _____

G. atlas _____

H. tantalizing _____

I. titanic _____

J. promethean _____

Middle School Language Arts Challenge
© The Learning Works, Inc.

Daffy Definitions

To the teacher: Have students form teams of four. Assign each team a word from the list below. Have the students on each team write a definition for the assigned word. One team at a time, mix up the student-created definitions with the actual definition and place them in a basket. At random, draw and read the definitions for each word. Let the class guess which is the dictionary definition.

arenaceous	resembling, containing, or made up of sand or sandy particles
epistrophe	the repetition of a word or words at the end of successive verses, phrases, or sentences ("of the people, by the people, for the people," for example)
mulligitawny	a soup, usually seasoned strongly with curry
myrmecology	the scientific study of ants
nosology	a branch of medical science that deals with the classification of diseases
picaroon	a pirate
sprag	a pointed stake or steel bar to let down from a wagon to keep it from rolling
spurtle	a wooden stick for stirring porridge
umiak	an open Eskimo boat made of a wooden frame covered with hide
verdigris	a greenish deposit found on copper, brass, or bronze

Have each team use a dictionary to come up with its own words!

Anagrams

An **anagram** is a new word or phrase created by changing the position of the letters in another word or phrase. For example, an anagram for the word *earth* is *heart*. The phrase *irate faces* is an anagram for the word *cafeterias*.

Write the definition for each of the following words. Then create an anagram from the letters in each word.

1. abashed
2. articulate
3. effusive
4. finagle

5. mendacity
6. plasticine
7. recumbent
8. variegated

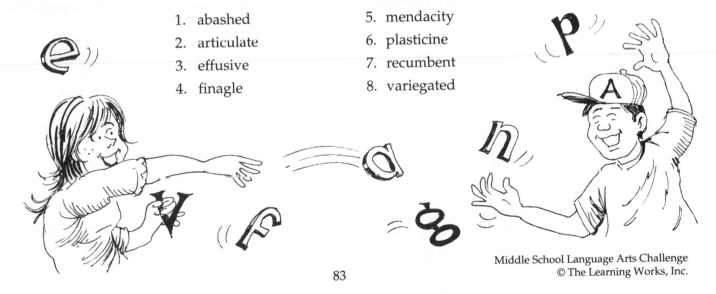

Middle School Language Arts Challenge
© The Learning Works, Inc.

Syllable Stretch

Use a dictionary to find as many five-syllable words as you can. Beside each word, write its definition. Then use it in a sentence.

Make a similar list of six-syllable words, seven-syllable words, and eight-syllable words with their definitions and a sentence for each. What words can you find with more than eight syllables?

Say "Aa"

Aa is a rough, scoriaceous lava. Use a dictionary to find as many other words as you can that begin and end with the letter *a*. Write the definition for each word.

What words can you find that begin and end with the letters *h*, *l*, *m*, *n*, and *t*? List as many as you can for each letter and write their definitions.

Select five of the most interesting words and write sentences using those words.

Middle School Language Arts Challenge
© The Learning Works, Inc.

Measured Words

List as many items as you can that might be used to measure something. For example, a *clock* measures *time*, a *metronome* measures *rhythm*, and an *altimeter* measures *altitude*.

Be creative in your thinking. Lists will be read aloud in class, and you will get one point for every word on your list that is not duplicated on another list.

A Good Reading Vocabulary

Make a list of things you can read. For example, you can read an **anthology** of poetry, a mathematical **formula**, and a funny **riddle**. Be creative, and be prepared to **read** your list to the class. You will receive a point for every word you have that no one else has listed.

Middle School Language Arts Challenge
© The Learning Works, Inc.

Food for Thought

How many of these "food words" can you describe? Write what you think would be a good definition for at least twelve of the words below. Then use a dictionary to check your definition and to look up the definitions for the words you don't know. What other unusual words can you list that describe edible things?

ambrosia	endive	kreplach
anise	escargot	kumquat
baklava	fennel	marzipan
béchamel	filbert	napoleon
casaba	flan	piccalilli
chorizo	frangipane	rutabaga
costard	gherkin	sapodilla
couscous	goulash	vichyssoise
damson	kohlrabi	whey

Public Speaking
and Drama

Instant Debates

To the teacher: *Assign a statement from the list below. Select students to argue in favor of and against the issue. Allow each student five minutes to prepare and two minutes to present his or her argument.*

The voting age should be lowered to 16.

Schools should have dress codes.

Smoking cigarettes should be illegal.

If a student gets in trouble in school, an effective consequence is to have the student's parents attend class with him or her for a day.

"America the Beautiful" should replace "The Star Spangled Banner" as the American national anthem.

What If?

To the teacher: *Assign the topics below to individual students or to groups of students. Encourage them to use their imaginations to predict what might happen in the situation assigned to them. Allow 60 seconds for each student to present his or her ideas to the class.*

What if. . .

kids were required to live at school from the age of six?

you moved to a country where you did not know the language?

your parents asked you to plan the ideal summer vacation for your family?

you could make yourself invisible?

your sense of hearing suddenly became extremely sensitive?

you were offered an opportunity to train for an Olympic team?

the local chamber of commerce asked you to organize a teen tour of your town?

Middle School Language Arts Challenge
© The Learning Works, Inc.

Improv

To the teacher: Have two students come to the front of the class. Select a situation from the list on page 94, or ask students for suggestions, and assign a role to each student. Call out a kind of action or an emotion for each student/character to act out (see page 95, or ask students for suggestions). Call out a new action to each student every few seconds.

Example:

You assign Mark the role of a fourteen-year-old son and tell Sarah to be his mother. You give them the situation of discussing Mark's poor report card.

Teacher: Sarah, you are angry. Mark, you are impatient.

Sarah: What a horrible report card! I told you this would happen! You've been goofing off all quarter!

Mark: Mom, will you get this over with? I told you I was sorry! My friends are waiting!

Improv

(continued)

Teacher: Sarah, now you're timid; Mark, you're helpless.

Sarah: Gee, I'm sorry, Mark. Have I held you up? I didn't mean to make you late. And those grades—don't worry about them. I'm sure you didn't mean to get an F in six subjects. Oh, dear, have I upset you mentioning those F's?

Mark: Oh, Mom, I just don't know what to do. Those teachers! They just keep assigning work! I can't keep up. How's a guy supposed to play video games, talk on the phone, watch TV, *and* study for some stupid test?

Teacher: Sarah—ecstatic; Mark—immature.

Sarah: Gee, Mark! These grades could be so much worse! Why, look at this comment from the school counselor. She says you find your way to class almost every time. Oh, Mark, I'm so proud!

Mark: Well, what'd you expect? DUH! And who cares about all those gross grades anyway? DUH! I'm gonna major in recess when I grow up, so I can play and play and play!

Middle School Language Arts Challenge
© The Learning Works, Inc.

Ideas for Improv Situations

Situations	Roles
taking a flight on a small airplane	father & twelve-year-old daughter
going to an expensive restaurant	teenage sister & three-year-old brother
auditioning for the school play	teenage girl & best friend
practicing before the big game	basketball coach & star player
discussing homework not turned in	math teacher & student
going to the orthodontist	mother & teenage daughter
working together on a school assignment: the history of arm wrestling in America	class brain & class cut-up
calling for a date	teenage boy & teenage girl
sitting in detention	teacher & teenage girl
creating a monster	scientist & assistant
watching a horror movie	six-year-old boy & mother
decorating a cake for a famous actor	baker & assistant
campaigning	presidential candidate & voter

Add your own ideas to the list or get suggestions from the class.

Ideas for Improv Actions

Student #1	Student #2	Student #1	Student #2
angry	excited	psychotic	prissy
timid	impatient	brilliant	distracted
curious	immature	elegant	forgetful
frightened	nervous	unimaginative	disappointed
helpless	devastated	willful	eager
aggressive	mischievous	formal	cheerful
annoyed	suspicious	exhausted	defiant
furious	evil	whining	sleepy
sweet	stingy	aggravated	grateful
joyous	hesitant	generous	mysterious

Add your own ideas to the list or get suggestions from the class.

Middle School Language Arts Challenge
© The Learning Works, Inc.

Extemporaneous Skits

To the teacher: Divide the class into groups of two or three. Assign each group a situation. Allow enough time for the group to assign roles and to sketch out the interaction of the characters in the skit. Then have the groups perform their skits for one another. If there is time, let the groups portray both a successful and an unsuccessful approach to resolving the problem posed.

Your friend tells you he has a copy of the history final, and he wants to give it to you. He plans to study it before the exam, which is next week. Your teacher walks in while you are talking.

You are with a friend who starts to talk about Carla, another friend of yours. She says Carla is snobbish and conceited. She says Carla has said things about you behind your back. Just then Carla walks up.

You and a friend are at the mall. You pay for a shirt, and the clerk gives you change for a twenty dollar bill when you have only given him a ten dollar bill. As you walk away, you realize the mistake. Your friend thinks you should keep the money.

You go out for pizza with a friend and his mother. While you are at the pizza parlor, your friend's mother drinks a pitcher of beer. Now it is time to go home, and you are concerned about riding home in the car with your friend's mom.

Extemporaneous Skits

(continued)

At your birthday party, one friend gives you a five-dollar gift certificate and another gives you a very expensive jacket.

You have a friend over. Your mom calls you into the kitchen to help her for a minute. When you return, you find your friend going through your mom's purse.

While you were at the public library a month ago, you borrowed your friend's library card to check out a book. The book is now past due, and you cannot find it. Your friend is at the door so you can go to the library to work on a school project together.

Your friend's family has invited you to celebrate a holiday with them. As part of the celebration, it is customary to eat fried beetles. You don't want to offend your friend, but you don't think you can eat the beetles. You are about to sit down at the table.

You have made poor math grades all year. On the last test, you received a perfect score. Your teacher accuses you of cheating by copying another student's answers. You didn't cheat.

You are at the shopping mall with your best friend, who whispers that he has just taken a pair of sunglasses and put them in his backpack. He wants to get out of the store before the clerk at the counter suspects him and searches his backpack.

Middle School Language Arts Challenge
© The Learning Works, Inc.

Future Digs

You are an archaeologist of the future. You are thrilled to discover the fabulous Lost Teen City of the 1990s. Hold up examples of the artifacts you have found and describe them to the audience before you. Explain how you think these artifacts might have been used by teenagers of the '90s. Remember, you are guessing their use based on their shape, color, size, and other physical clues. Here are some suggested artifacts, but feel free to think of others.

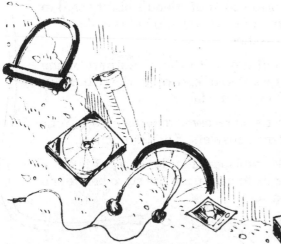

a compact disc

a bicycle lock

an in-line skate

headphones

protective kneepad

a baseball card

a disposable camera

an empty three-ring binder

dental floss

What's My Bag?

To the teacher: *Have each student bring in a paper bag with six or seven items inside. Every item must have at least one characteristic in common.*

For example, a bag containing a dog's leash, a safety pin, a hole punch, a piece of round cereal, a piece of macaroni, and a nylon stocking with the toe worn through would be a bag of **things with holes**.

Have the students, in turn, hold up the items in their bags one at a time, while the other students guess what the items have in common. Award points or certificates to any student who can stump the class.

Middle School Language Arts Challenge
© The Learning Works, Inc.

Power of Persuasion

You have been given two minutes to try to persuade the faculty and administration of your school to approve a new program or privilege for the students. Use one of the ideas listed below, or think of one of your own. Support your argument with as many facts as you can. You may use props or ask witnesses to speak if it will make your argument more convincing or appealing.

Lockers should be equipped with small refrigerators.

A class field trip to a ski resort would be educational and worthwhile.

The school should offer a course called "The History of Video Games."

Students want to organize a fund-raiser for which a controversial rock musician has offered to perform.

School should be dismissed early during World Series games.

A student wants to bring his dog to class every day.

Games and
Challenges

Decipher

In the puzzles below, only the initials of the key words have been given. Write the key words to complete each phrase.

1. 88 K on a P
2. 29 D in F in a LY
3. 9 P in the SS
4. 9 J on the USSC
5. 50 S on the AF
6. 100 Y in a C
7. 206 B in the HB
8. 360 D in a C
9. G and the 3 B
10. 100 P in a D

11. 13 OC
12. 1,000 M in a K
13. 9 P on a BT
14. 8 T on an O
15. 90 D in a RA
16. 3 W on a T
17. 1,001 AN
18. 3 S and YO
19. 2 P in a Q
20. 24 H in a D

Make up ten decipher puzzles of your own and see if you can stump the class.

Rail Fence Code

Send messages to your friends in code. One kind of code is shown here.

To use the rail fence code, write alternate letters of the message in one row and the other letters in a second row so that the letters are staggered.

Message: Meet me at the movies.

1. M E M A T E O I S
      E T E T H M V E

Next, compress the letters in the first row. Then compress the letters in the second row and write them beside the letters in the first row.

2. MEMATEOIS ETETHMVE

Finally, divide this single row of letters into groups of four letters each. Use any letter or letters you like to fill up the final letter group.

3. MEMA TEOI SETE TIIMV ELAR

Decipher this message: SIET HTAH RMLA TEEC EYRL

Middle School Language Arts Challenge
© The Learning Works, Inc.

Ever, Ever Eve

A **palindrome** is a word or phrase that reads the same from left to right and right to left. A famous palindrome is "Madam, I'm Adam."

Other palindromes:

> Able I was ere I saw Elba.
> A dog—a panic in a pagoda!
> A man, a plan, a canal—Panama!
> Too hot to hoot.
> Was it a cat I saw?

Using at least ten letters, create your own palindrome.

Reversals

Some words become other words when their letters are reversed. For example, *deliver* becomes *reviled*, and *live* becomes *evil*. List as many "reversal" words as you can.

Middle School Language Arts Challenge
© The Learning Works, Inc.

It's Symbolic

A **symbol** is a sign, picture, or mark that stands for something else. Describe the meaning of each of the following symbols. Look up any symbols you do not know.

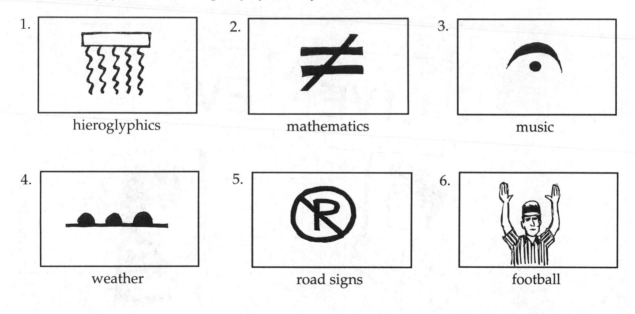

1. hieroglyphics

2. mathematics

3. music

4. weather

5. road signs

6. football

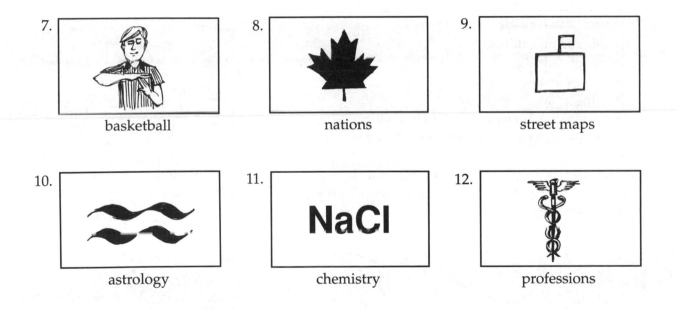

7. basketball

8. nations

9. street maps

10. astrology

11. NaCl — chemistry

12. professions

Lists of Lists

Make a separate list of words and phrases to fit each of the following descriptions:

- things that bustle
- things that rustle
- things you can flip
- things that slip
- things that are intense
- things that are immense
- things that are round but do not bounce
- things that are green but do not grow

Be as descriptive as you can in making your lists. For example, something that would slip might be "colored sprinkles atop a melting scoop." Have fun. If you have time, make up your own categories for lists.

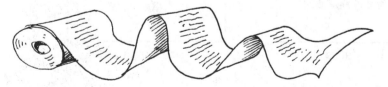

What's in a Name?

Sometimes people have names that seem to suit their occupations. Sally Ride, for example, is a famous astronaut. Rollie Fingers was a famous baseball pitcher. A judge might be named Justice, or a banker might be named Teller.

Create some suitable names for the occupations listed below. Then use three of the people you have named as characters in a dialogue or short story.

veterinarian	marine biologist	poet
lion tamer	chef	truck driver
banker	waiter	pediatrician
real estate salesperson	telephone operator	pilot
teacher	accountant	artist

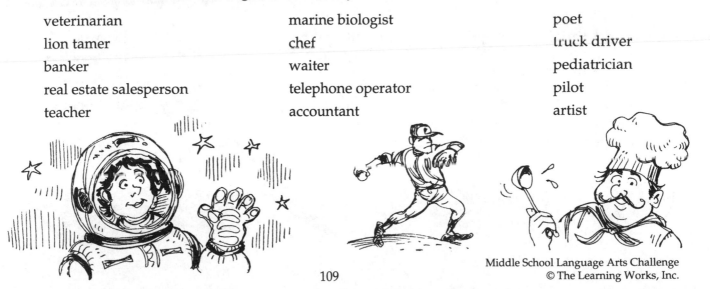

Middle School Language Arts Challenge
© The Learning Works, Inc.

The Union Jack

Although both the British and American people speak English, there are many words that are uniquely British. Can you name the American word or expression that means the same as the following British words and expressions?

1. lorry
2. tights
3. grips
4. car park
5. gangway
6. cot
7. lie in

8. fringe
9. back garden
10. gone off
11. lift
12. the lot
13. nappy
14. cotton

15. pavement
16. petrol
17. torch
18. wool
19. boot
20. pop in
21. bonnet

Pangram Puzzlers

A **pangram** is a sentence that contains all the letters of the alphabet, repeating as few letters as possible.

For example, *A quick brown fox jumped over the lazy dogs.*
In this sentence, all twenty-six letters are used and only four letters are repeated.

Write a pangram of your own with as few letter repetitions as possible.

111

Tom Swiftly

Tom Swift was a fictional boy inventor who created all kinds of wild contraptions. The Tom Swift books were written in a style that has been imitated by pairing a character's quote with an adverb that creates a pun.

For example, *"Have some more ice cream," she said coldly.*

"He's not too bright," I said blankly.

"I think I'll sharpen my pencil," Dave said pointedly.

Have fun creating your own "Tom Swiftly" quotes and reading them aloud to your class.

Musical Words

The notes of the musical scale are *A, B, C, D, E, F,* and *G.* Make as many words as you can that use only these seven letters. In each word, you may repeat any letter as many times as you wish, but you may use only the seven letters of the musical scale.

Examples: *gabbed, edge, faded, baggage, face*

Share your list of words with the class. You will receive a point for each word you found that is on no one else's list.

Middle School Language Arts Challenge
© The Learning Works, Inc.

All Groan Up

A **pun** is a humorous use of words that sound alike or nearly alike but have different meanings.

Examples: The two spiders who got married were happy newly webs.

Have you seen the dolphin fountain in Santa Barbara? It spouts water on porpoise.

Create ten original puns of your own. Use these words that sound similar, or choose your own. Have a pun-derful time!

suite/sweet	Shirley/surely
altar/alter	umpire/empire
pain/pane	steal/steel
soar/sore	cent/scent
knight/night	puddle/poodle

ANSWER KEY

Cast of Characters—page 8

1. *A Christmas Carol* by Charles Dickens
2. *The Secret Garden* by Frances Hodgson Burnett
3. *The Adventures of Tom Sawyer* by Mark Twain
4. *The Cay* by Theodore Taylor
5. *A Wrinkle in Time* by Madeleine L'Engle
6. *James and the Giant Peach* by Roald Dahl
7. *To Kill a Mockingbird* by Harper Lee
8. *Little Women* by Louisa May Alcott
9. *Rebecca of Sunnybrook Farm* by Kate Douglas Wiggin
10. *Twenty Thousand Leagues Under the Sea* by Jules Verne
11. *A Separate Peace* by John Knowles
12. *The Outsiders* by S. E. Hinton
13. *Oliver Twist* by Charles Dickens
14. *Wutership Down* by Richard Adams
15. *The Last of the Mohicans* by James Fenimore Cooper

Villainous Villains—page 9

1. Smaug
2. the White Witch
3. Captain James Hook, in *Peter Pan* by J. M. Barrie
4. Cluny the Scourge
5. Long John Silver
6. Simon Legree
7. Mr. Hyde, of *Dr. Jekyll and Mr. Hyde* by Robert Louis Stevenson
8. Uriah Heep
9. the Horned King
10. Professor Moriarty

Middle School Language Arts Challenge
© The Learning Works, Inc.

ANSWER KEY

Who Said That?—page 10

1. Anne Frank, in *Anne Frank: The Diary of a Young Girl*
2. Phillip Enright, in *The Cay* by Theodore Taylor
3. The Grand High Witch, in *The Witches* by Roald Dahl
4. Alice, in *Alice's Adventures in Wonderland* by Lewis Carroll
5. Beth, in *Little Women* by Louisa May Alcott
6. Pollyanna, in *Pollyanna* by Eleanor H. Porter
7. Tom Sawyer, in *The Adventures of Tom Sawyer* by Mark Twain
8. Sherlock Holmes, in *The Hound of the Baskervilles* by Sir Arthur Conan Doyle
9. Romeo, in *Romeo and Juliet* by William Shakespeare
10. Anne, in *Anne of Green Gables* by L. M. Montgomery

Who Am I?—page 11

1. Maniac Magee, from *Maniac Magee* by Jerry Spinelli
2. Shirley Temple Wong (also known as Sixth Cousin or Bandit), from *In the Year of the Boar and Jackie Robinson* by Bette Bao Lord
3. Mafatu, or Stout Heart, from *Call It Courage* by Armstrong Sperry
4. M. C. Higgins, from *M. C. Higgins, the Great* by Virginia Hamilton
5. Phillip Malloy, from *Nothing But the Truth* by Avi

ANSWER KEY

Famous Settings—page 12

1. *The Secret Garden* by Frances Hodgson Burnett
2. *The Twenty-One Balloons* by William Pène du Bois
3. *Mary Poppins* by P. L. Travers
4. *Homer Price* by Robert McClosky
5. *From the Mixed-Up Files of Mrs. Basil E. Frankweiler* by E. L. Konigsburg
6. *Tuck Everlasting* by Natalie Babbitt
7. *The True Confessions of Charlotte Doyle* by Avi
8. *The House of Dies Drear* by Virginia Hamilton
9. *Shoeless Joe* by W. P. Kinsella
10. *The Slave Dancer* by Paula Fox
11. *Arabian Nights*, author unknown
12. *Sarah Bishop* by Scott O'Dell
13. the Sherlock Holmes stories by Sir Arthur Conan Doyle
14. *Gone with the Wind* by Margaret Mitchell
15. *Jane Eyre* by Charlotte Brontë

Literary Geography—page 13

1. Canada
2. Vietnam
3. New York
4. Mississippi
5. Prince Edward Island, Canada
6. Switzerland
7. Alaska
8. Japan
9. Wisconsin
10. Holland
11. Hungary
12. Scotland
13. Mexico
14. South Africa
15. China

Throughout History—pages 14-15

1. *Across Five Aprils* by Irene Hunt
2. *The Fighting Ground* by Avi
3. *Number the Stars* by Lois Lowry
4. *The Slave Dancer* by Paula Fox

Middle School Language Arts Challenge
© The Learning Works, Inc.

ANSWER KEY

5. *Johnny Tremain* by Esther Forbes
6. *Island of the Blue Dolphins* by Scott O'Dell
7. *By the Great Horn Spoon!* by Sid Fleischman
8. *Naya Nuki: Girl Who Ran* by Kenneth Thomasma
9. *Dragonwings* by Laurence Yep
10. *A Gathering of Days: A New England Girl's Journal, 1830-32* by Joan Blos
11. *Adam of the Road* by Elizabeth Janet Gray
12. *The Master Puppeteer* by Katherine Paterson
13. *Roll of Thunder, Hear My Cry* by Mildred Taylor
14. *Farewell to Manzanar* by Jeanne Wakatsuki Houston and James D. Houston
15. *Kidnapped* by Robert Louis Stevenson

Memorable Leads—pages 16-17

1. *A Wind in the Door* by Madeleine L'Engle
2. *Peter Pan* by J. M. Barrie
3. *Hatchet* by Gary Paulsen
4. *The Adventures of Huckleberry Finn* by Mark Twain
5. *Julie of the Wolves* by Jean Craighead George
6. *Redwall* by Brian Jacques

7. *The Incredible Journey* by Sheila Burnford
8. *A Gathering of Days: A New England Girl's Journal, 1830-32* by Joan W. Blos
9. *Tell Me That You Love Me, Junie Moon* by Marjorie Kellogg
10. *The Grapes of Wrath* by John Steinbeck

Name That Author—page 18

1. Marjorie K. Rawlings
2. Mildred Taylor
3. Kate Douglas Wiggin
4. Robert C. O'Brien
5. Felix Salten
6. Ray Bradbury
7. Mary Mapes Dodge
8. Walter Dean Myers
9. Betty Smith
10. Robert Louis Stevenson
11. Robert Cormier
12. Robin McKinley
13. Madeleine L'Engle
14. Katherine Paterson
15. Chaim Potok
16. Helen Hunt Jackson

ANSWER KEY

Literary Aliases—page 19
1. Mark Twain
2. O. Henry
3. Dr. Seuss
4. Lewis Carroll
5. John Le Carré (As a diplomat in the British Foreign Service, he was forbidden to publish under his own name.)
6. George Orwell
7. Agatha Christie
8. Charles Dickens
9. Benjamin Franklin
10. Washington Irving

Series of Series—page 20
1. Lloyd Alexander
2. C. S. Lewis
3. Beverly Cleary
4. Anne McCaffrey
5. Walter Farley
6. Joan Lowry Nixon
7. L. Frank Baum
8. Agatha Christie
9. Agatha Christie
10. Sir Arthur Conan Doyle

11. J. R. R. Tolkien
12. Susan Cooper
13. John Christopher
14. James Fenimore Cooper
15. Isaac Asimov

Animals in Literature—page 21
1. Wilbur, in *Charlotte's Web* by E. B. White
2. Black Star, in *Black Star, Bright Dawn* by Scott O'Dell
3. Stickly-Prickly Hedgehog and Slow-Solid Tortoise, in *Just So Stories* by Rudyard Kipling
4. White Fang, in *White Fang* by Jack London
5. Winnie-the-Pooh, in *Winnie-the-Pooh* and *The House at Pooh Corner* by A. A. Milne
6. Napoleon and Snowball, in *Animal Farm* by George Orwell
7. Cheshire Cat, in *Alice's Adventures in Wonderland* by Lewis Carroll
8. Piebald, in *"National Velvet"* by Enid Bagnold
9. Old Yeller, in *Old Yeller* by Fred Gibson
10. Old Dan and Little Ann, in *Where the Red Fern Grows* by Wilson Rawls

Middle School Language Arts Challenge
© The Learning Works, Inc.

ANSWER KEY

Animal Titles—page 22
1. *Lion*
2. *Dolphins*
3. *Pigs*
4. *Monkeys*
5. *Wolves*
6. *Cat*
7. *Swans*
8. *Hawk*
9. *Mockingbird*
10. *Fish*

Book Bouquets—page 23
1. *Daisy*
2. *Rose*
3. *Willows*
4. *Rose*
5. *Tree*
6. *Tree*
7. *Cherry Tree*
8. *Chrysanthemum*
9. *Tree*
10. *Poplars*

11. *Tree*
12. *Dandelion*
13. *Flowers*
14. *Lilies*
15. *Garden*

Devouring a Good Book—page 24
1. *Strawberry*
2. *Bagels*
3. *Peach*
4. *Popcorn, Buttermilk*
5. *Tomatoes*
6. *Chocolate*
7. *Sugar*
8. *Scrambled Eggs*
9. *Onion*
10. *Peppers*
11. *Potato*
12. *Vegetable*
13. *Peppermint*
14. *Grapes*
15. *Sugar*

ANSWER KEY

Colorful Literature—page 25

1. Elizabeth George Speare
2. Brian Jacques
3. Cynthia Voigt
4. Scott O'Dell
5. John Steinbeck
6. Eleanor Estes
7. L. M. Montgomery
8. Walter Farley
9. Scott O'Dell
10. John Christopher
11. Jim Kjelgaard
12. Lucy M. Boston
13. Susan Cooper
14. Wilson Rawls
15. Mary O'Hara

Poetic Quotes—page 26

1. "Stopping by Woods on a Snowy Evening" by Robert Frost
2. "There Is No Frigate Like a Book" by Emily Dickinson
3. "The Fog" by Carl Sandberg
4. "Hug O' War" by Shel Silverstein
5. "The Village Blacksmith" by Henry Wadsworth Longfellow
6. "Casey at the Bat" by Ernest Lawrence Thayer
7. "The Negro Speaks of Rivers" by Langston Hughes

The first poet to participate in a presidential inauguration was Robert Frost (the inauguration of John F. Kennedy in 1961).

The Extraordinary Newbery—page 27

1. E
2. G
3. A
4. F
5. J
6. B
7. D
8. C
9. H
10. I

Middle School Language Arts Challenge
© The Learning Works, Inc.

ANSWER KEY

More Newbery—page 28

1. D.   6. A
2. H   7. C
3. B   8. E
4. G   9. F
5. J   10. I

The winner of the first Newbery Award was *The Story of Mankind* by Hendrik Van Loon.

Literary Trivia—pages 29-30

1. L. M. Montgomery, author of *Anne of Green Gables, Anne of Avonlea*, etc.
2. Henry Wadsworth Longfellow
3. John Steinbeck
4. Walter Farley
5. Pippi Longstocking
6. Madeleine L'Engle
7. Louisa May Alcott
8. Charles Dickens
9. Sir Arthur Conan Doyle; the character was Sherlock Holmes
10. Emily Dickinson
11. Rudyard Kipling
12. Mark Twain
13. Robert Frost
14. S. E. Hinton
15. Oz; the file cabinet was marked "O-Z"

Authors with Challenges—page 31

1. Ernest Hemingway
2. Robert Louis Stevenson
3. Hans Christian Anderson
4. Mark Twain
5. Charles Dickens
6. Emily and Charlotte Brontë
7. Aldous Huxley
8. Jean Little

Odd Jobs—page 32

1. E   7. D
2. B   8. C
3. G   9. K
4. J   10. I
5. L   11. F
6. A   12. H

ANSWER KEY

Extra! Extra!—page 46

1.	C	6.	H	
2.	F	7.	J	
3.	I	8.	E	
4.	D	9.	G	
5.	A	10.	B	

Pesky Apostrophes—pages 54

It's surprising to me that kids today don't read more of Mark Twain's novels. After you've read his tales of the Mississippi, you'll find yourself laughing at all of his characters' wild adventures. Maybe one of the problems kids have with Twain's books is deciding how many p's, i's, and s's to put in all those *Mississippi's* they have to write in their reports. There's a way around that, though, if you're creative. In Jamal's report on *The Adventures of Huckleberry Finn*, Jamal counted four i's, four s's, and two p's each time he used the word *Mississippi*. Claryce's solution was to refer to "that big, muddy river," avoiding the problem altogether!

Periods and Commas—page 55

Although Kevin was normally on time, today he was going to be late. First, his alarm didn't go off. Next, the shower was out of hot water. Finally, as he sat down to breakfast, he spilled his cereal on the floor. He went to the garage to get a broom, and the back door closed behind him. He was locked out, and the only way into the house was through the dog door. As he crawled through the tiny door, his dog, Pavlov, licked Kevin's face, neck, and hands. Kevin was beginning to think this awful, frustrating morning would never end!

A Plethora of Plurals—page 56

1.	oxen	9.	cactuses or cacti
2.	data	10.	mothers-in-law
3.	passersby	11.	moose
4.	potatoes	12.	lice
5.	comedies	13.	crises
6.	alumni	14.	halves
7.	alumnae	15.	algae
8.	dice		

Middle School Language Arts Challenge
© The Learning Works, Inc.

ANSWER KEY

A Capital Idea—page 57

When **I** went to Washington, **D.C.**, with my family over **s**pring **b**reak, I saw many interesting sights. In **M**ay, the **c**herry **b**lossoms are in bloom, and **I** took lots of pictures with my new **p**ocket-sized **c**amera. My favorite **m**onument was the Jefferson **M**emorial, although my **s**ister liked the **C**apitol best. **W**e even met our **s**enator, **L**otta **V**otz, who arranged a tour of the **W**hite **H**ouse for us. **W**e did not, however, meet **P**resident **P**artisan, who was touring the **F**ar **E**ast with the **s**ecretary of **s**tate.

Misplaced Modifiers—page 58

1. President Lincoln wrote the Gettysburg Address **on the back of an envelope** while he was traveling.
2. Jessica broke her leg **in three places** while she was skiing.
3. Rosie, **who was trying out for the varsity team,** pitched baseballs to her dog.
4. The orthodontist adjusted Katherine's braces **with a sharp twist**.
5. I caught the ball **dropping from the sky**.

They're, Their, There—page 59

1. stationery, loose
2. poor, it's, dessert, dinner, their
3. mayor, your, advice, site, new, capitol, mall
4. through, already, past, toll
5. accept, principles, illicit
6. proceed, moral, course, course, than, conscience
7. would have, effect, too

ANSWER KEY

In Agreement—page 60
1. drives
2. are
3. is
4. watches
5. yells
6. arrives
7. waits
8. was
9. was
10. was

Agreeable Pronouns—page 61
1. his
2. I
3. himself
4. his
5. me
6. her
7. themselves
8. his
9. I
10. She
11. Whom
12. Who

Regularly Irregular—pages 62-63
1. knew, lent
2. strode
3. sprang or sprung, swung
4. set, wrung, wept
5. froze, wished, fled, saw, arose
6. laid, clung
7. crept, burst
8. slid, swore

Proof It—page 65

1. pat threw the ball from second to first base to complete the double play for the tolers.

2. when she returned her to desk cathy found the homework sheet thought she lost had.

3. the principle of litle mountian school called mary, rosa, and todd to the office for important meeting.

4. scotts mother begged him to change the radio station.

5. the boys lost the soccer game at recess.

Middle School Language Arts Challenge
© The Learning Works, Inc.

ANSWER KEY

Dynamite Diagrams—page 67

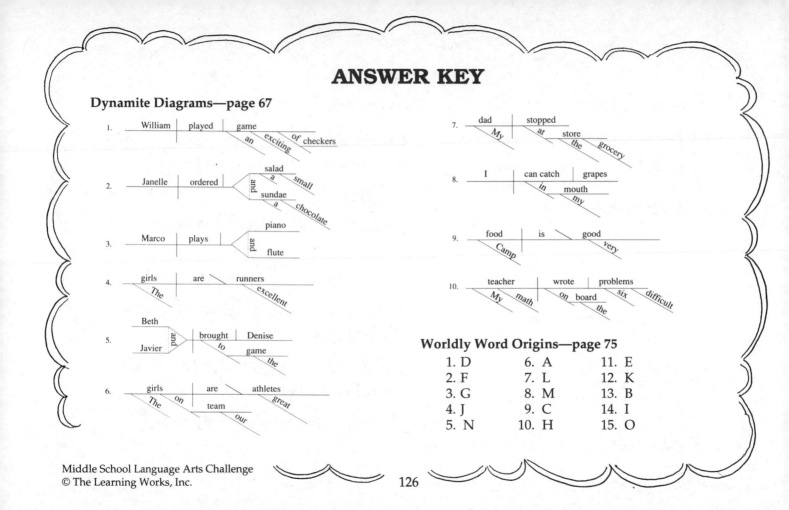

1. William | played | game
   an exciting / of checkers

2. Janelle | ordered
   salad (a) small
   and
   sundae (a) chocolate

3. Marco | plays
   piano
   and
   flute

4. girls | are \ runners
   The excellent

5. Beth and Javier | brought | Denise
   to game the

6. girls | are \ athletes
   The on great
   team our

7. dad | stopped
   My at store
   the grocery

8. I | can catch | grapes
   in mouth my

9. food | is \ good
   Camp very

10. teacher | wrote | problems
    My math on board six difficult
    the

Worldly Word Origins—page 75

1. D
2. F
3. G
4. J
5. N
6. A
7. L
8. M
9. C
10. H
11. E
12. K
13. B
14. I
15. O

ANSWER KEY

Namesakes—page 76

1. guillotine
2. pasteurize or pasteurization
3. bowdlerize
4. poinsettia
5. chauvinism
6. nicotine
7. saxophone
8. mesmerize
9. Levi's
10. sideburns

Occupations—page 77

1. D
2. H
3. C
4. F
5. B
6. A
7. G
8. E
9. I
10. J

The Hobbyist—page 78

1. I
2. C
3. F
4. A
5. B
6. D
7. E
8. J
9. H
10. G

Don't Myth Out—page 81

1. C, Narcissus
2. G, Atlas
3. E, Mars
4. A, Ceres
5. J, Prometheus
6. B, Pan
7. H, Tantalus
8. I, the Titans
9. D, Vulcan
10. F, Hercules

Anagrams—page 83

Answers will vary. An example of one anagram for each word is listed:

1. bead ash
2. acute trail
3. five fuse
4. leafing
5. mint decay
6. incite pals
7. teen crumb
8. give a trade

Decipher—page 102

1. 88 Keys on a Piano
2. 29 Days in February in a Leap Year
3. 9 Planets in the Solar System
4. 9 Justices on the U.S. Supreme Court
5. 50 Stars on the American Flag
6. 100 Years in a Century
7. 206 Bones in the Human Body
8. 360 Degrees in a Circle
9. Goldilocks and the 3 Bears
10. 100 Pennies in a Dollar

Middle School Language Arts Challenge
© The Learning Works, Inc.

ANSWER KEY

11. 13 Original Colonies
12. 1,000 Meters in a Kilometer
13. 9 Players on a Baseball Team
14. 8 Tentacles on an Octopus
15. 90 Degrees in a Right Angle
16. 3 Wheels on a Tricycle
17. 1,001 Arabian Nights
18. 3 Strikes and You're Out
19. 2 Pints in a Quart
20. 24 Hours in a Day

Rail Fence Code—page 103

1. Smile at the teacher.

It's Symbolic—pages 106-107

1. rain
2. not equal
3. hold or pause
4. warm front
5. no parking
6. touchdown or field goal
7. technical foul

8. Canada
9. school
10. Aquarius
11. salt
12. medicine

The Union Jack—page 110

1. truck
2. panty hose
3. luggage
4. garage
5. aisle
6. crib
7. sleep late
8. bangs
9. back yard
10. spoiled
11. elevator
12. all
13. diaper
14. thread
15. sidewalk
16. gasoline
17. flashlight
18. yarn
19. trunk
20. drop by
21. hood (of a car)